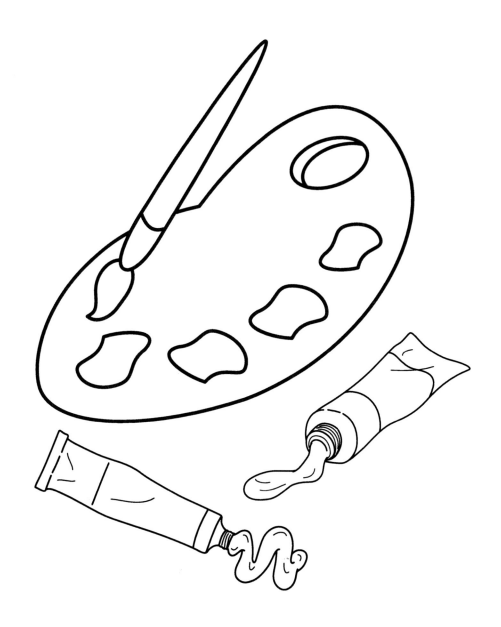

# Welcome to Watercolor Painting!

## Materials you will need:

- Watercolor paints in tubes
- Watercolor paper (100% cotton if possible)
- Watercolor paint brushes in different sizes
- Palette for mixing paints
- Spray bottle of water for wetting paper
- Cup of water for cleaning brushes
- Paper towels

Watercolor painting can be messy (and don't let the name of the paint fool you), watercolors can stain fabric - be careful!

## Basic technique - wet-on-wet:

- Use spray bottle or paint brush to wet watercolor paper with clean water.
- Mix pea size dot of paint with a few drops of water on palette.
- Apply paint to wet paper using wet paintbrush.
- Allow paint to spread.

Try something like these watercolor flowers. See how the colors "bleed" in to the paper and in to each other?

## Basic technique - wet-on-dry:

- Get a dry piece of watercolor paper.
- Place a pea size drop of paint into the paint palette (only add water if paint is too thick).
- Use a wet brush to apply full strength paint to paper for designs with sharp edges.

Full strength watercolor on dry paper
makes it possible to draw cleaner edges
and can be more colorful!

## **Paint a simple landscape part#1:**

Let's begin with the sky.

- Use the spray bottle or paint brush to wet the top half of your paper.
- Mix a blue color or two with drops of water.
- Use wet paintbrush to apply a light blue "wash" for the sky, letting it blend naturally.

It can take up to 30 minutes for watercolor paper to dry completely - speed up the process by using a hairdryer!

## Paint a simple landscape part #2:

Next add mountains to dry paper.

- In your palette, mix some light brown paint with a drop of water.
- With a wet paintbrush, use the wet-on-dry technique to add a brown mountain shapes to the middle section of the painting.
- You can add several layers of mountains.

You can use a pencil to sketch out the mountain shapes before painting.

Use the edge of the brush to trace the edges of the mountains - and then drag your brush down and away from the line to blend the colors.

## Paint a simple landscape part #3:

How about adding a field of grass in the foreground?

- Start by mixing a few shades of green on your palette.
- Use the wet-on-dry method to add different shades of green to the bottom 1/3rd of the painting.
- Now use a small dry-on-dry brush (dry brush, dry paper) with short, upward strokes to add the texture of the grass.

You can add flowers to your grass by using the tip of the paintbrush and adding several dots.

You have just completed a watercolor landscape painting! Hop for joy!

## Simple details part #1:

Let's try some trees.

- Use a small round brush.
- Mix a dark brown paint color.
- Make several vertical tree trunks of trees and branches (wet-on-dry).
- Mix a few shades of green.
- "Dab" your brush to add the leaves (wet-on-dry).

Or try painting the leaves first, and then adding the trunks and branches on top like these trees here.

## Simple details part #2:

Let's add some water near the trees.

- Blend some blue and green paints in your palette with water.
- Wet the area of the paper you will be adding water to.
- Use the wet-on-wet technique like you did for the clouds to add a pond or river.

Try waving the brush from side to side to create ripples in the water!

## Simple details part #2:

Now it's time to try some highlights and shadows.

- Paint a simple object like an apple on a table.
- Use a lighter shade of paint in the areas that you want to highlight.
- Use a darker shade of paint for the areas that you want to have in shadow.

Notice the highlights on the right side of the apple and the shadow on the left. When painting, imagine where the light is coming from and paint highlights and shadows accordingly.

## Practice, practice, practice:

- Try experimenting with different color/water mixtures and paintbrushes.
- Try replicating simple objects you find around you. Focus on highlights and shading.
- Use a sketchbook with watercolor paper to practice - tear the paper out so it doesn't wet the whole book.

Use a light pencil to sketch or trace a
picture and then follow over the lines with
watercolor paint.

Set up a "still life" by grouping together objects on a table, add a light from one direction, and then use it for inspiration to paint!